Parts of a Flower

By Candice Ransom

Lerner Publications · Minneapolis

The images in this book are used with the permission of: © Lily Bokeh/David Gunter/Moment Open/ agency/Getty Images, p. 4; © iStockphoto.com/Flander, p. 5; © iStockphoto.com/Thomas Vogel, p. 6; © Lawren Lu/Alamy, p. 7; © ArminStautBerlin/iStock/Thinkstock, p. 8; © Medioimages/Photodisc/ Thinkstock, p. 9; © Valter Cunha/iStock/Thinkstock, p. 10; © Michael Neelon/Alamy, p. 11; © Universal Images Group Limited/Alamy, pp. 12, 13; © Handmade Pictures/iStock/Thinkstock, p. 14; © iStockphoto.com/haydynyah, p. 15; © iStockphoto.com/S847, p. 16; © iStockphoto.com/pixelnest, p. 17; © iStockphoto.com/proxyminder, p. 18; © Zoonar/Thinkstock, p. 19; © LilieGraphie/iStock/ Thinkstock, p. 20; © whitetag/iStock/Thinkstock, p. 21; © Frank Von Delft/Cultura/Getty Images, p. 22.

Front cover: © pigphoto/iStock/Thinkstock.

Main body text set in ITC Avant Garde Gothic Std Medium 21/25.
Typeface provided by Adobe Systems.

Lerner Publications Company
A division of Lerner Publishing Group, Inc.
241 First Avenue North
Minneapolis, MN 55401 USA

For reading levels and more information, look up this title at www.lernerbooks.com.

Library of Congress Cataloging-in-Publication Data

Ransom, Candice F., 1952–
     Parts of a flower / by Candice Ransom.
         pages   cm. — (First step nonfiction. Pollination)
     Includes index.
     ISBN 978–1–4677–5739–3 (lib. bdg. : alk. paper)
     ISBN 978–1–4677–6226–7 (eBook)
     1. Flowers—Anatomy—Juvenile literature. 2. Flowers—Juvenile literature. I. Title. II. Series:
First step nonfiction. Pollination.
     QK653.R36 2015
     581—dc23   2014014780

Manufactured in the United States of America
1 – CG – 12/31/14

Table of Contents

Plants Have Parts   4

Close-Up on Flowers   9

How Flower Parts Make Seeds   15

Glossary   23

Index   24

Plants Have Parts

Look at this flowering plant.

Leaves are one part of a plant.

All plants have many parts.

Plants take in water through roots.

Roots hold a plant in the ground.

This plant has thick stems.

Stems keep plants upright.

There's a flower peeking out of this bud!

Buds open into leaves and flowers.

Flowers are very important
parts of plants. Let's give
them a closer look.

This flower has
bright purple petals.

Flowers have many parts of
their own. All flowers have
petals.

This part of the
flower is male.

This part of
the flower
is female.

Most flowers have both male
and female parts. These
parts help make new plants.

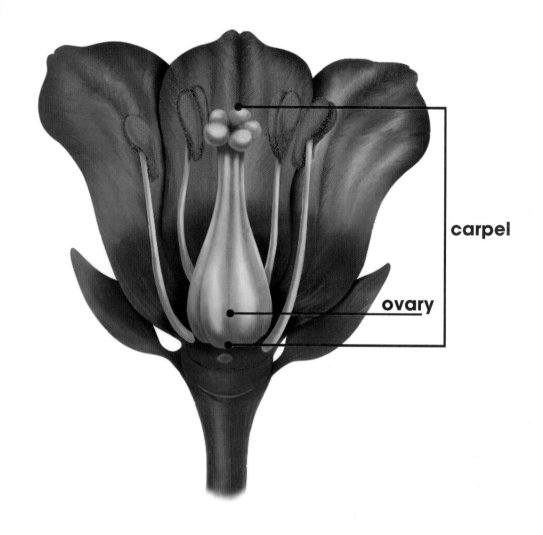

carpel

ovary

The female part of the
flower is the **carpel**. It
holds eggs in its **ovary**.

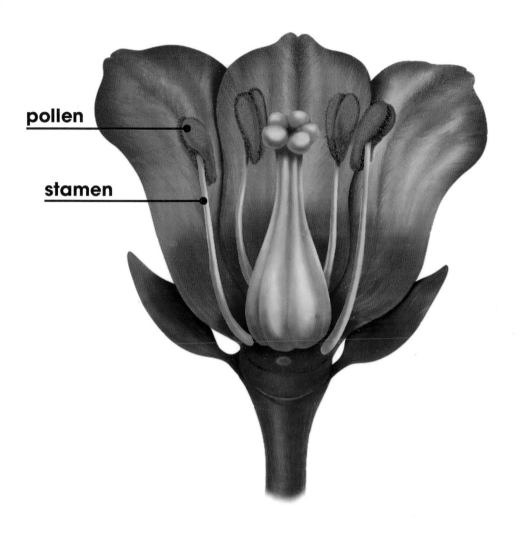

pollen

stamen

The male part of the flower is the **stamen**. **Pollen** gathers on the stamen.

13

These seeds came from a sunflower.

What do all these parts do? They make seeds!

How Flower Parts Make Seeds

pollen

These apple blossoms have yellow pollen on the stamen.

Flowers start making seeds when pollen moves from the stamen to the carpel. 15

Bees help pollinate apple blossoms. These flowers make fruit and seeds.

Pollen can get on the carpel with the help of insects such as bees. Bees are **pollinators**.

This bee is carrying pollen on its legs.

A bee flies from flower to flower gathering pollen. It stores pollen on its body.

Pollen on the bee's legs touches this apple blossom's carpel.

The pollen carried by the bee can rub off on the flower's carpel.

18

An apple blossom will make fruit and seeds when it is pollinated.

The pollen will join with eggs inside the ovary to make seeds.

Fruit will soon be growing on this apple tree.

Seeds usually form inside fruit.

When fruit is fully grown, it releases the seeds.

Seeds grow into new plants!

Glossary

buds – small growths on plant stems that later develop into leaves or flowers

carpel – the female part of a flower. The carpel holds eggs in its ovary.

ovary – the part of a flower's carpel where eggs grow

pollen – a powdery substance produced by a flower's stamen

pollinators – animals, humans, or wind that pollinate flowers

stamen – the male part of a flower

Index

buds – 8

carpel – 12, 15–16, 18

fruit – 20–21

ovary – 12, 19

petals – 10

pollen – 13, 15–19

seeds – 14–15, 19–22

stamen – 13, 15